SOAR ABOVE THE
MADNESS

Surviving Office Politics
Without Losing Your Mind,
Your Job, or Your Lunch

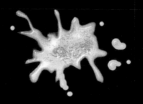

WRITTEN BY
MIRIAM DRENNAN

CREATED BY
JOEL ANDERSON

RUTLEDGE HILL PRESS®
Nashville, Tennessee

A Division of Thomas Nelson, Inc.
www.ThomasNelson.com

Published by Rutledge Hill Press, a division of Thomas Nelson, Inc., P.O. Box 141000, Nashville, Tennessee, 37214.

Library of Congress Cataloging-in-Publication Data

Drennan, Miriam, 1968–

 Soar above the madness: surviving office politics without losing your mind, your job, or your lunch / written by Miriam Drennan; created by Joel Anderson.

  p. cm.

 ISBN 1-55853-979-4

 1. Office politics. 2. Teams in the workplace. 3. Leadership. 4. Interpersonal communication. 5. Interpersonal relations. 6. Success in business. I. Anderson, Joel. II. Title.

HF5386.5 .D74 2002

650.1'3—dc21

2001058870

Printed in Italy

02 03 04 05 06—5 4 3 2 1

Table of Contents

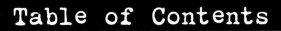

Thanks to all the strange bosses and odd coworkers who've ever had the joy of my presence. Without you, this book would not have been possible—and you know who you are. I'd also like to offer my compassion to the good bosses and nice coworkers who've had to put up with me—and bless your hearts, you know who you are, too.

Joel, just in case you're wondering, you fall into the latter category. Thanks for believing in me; you are, and continue to be, a blessing in my life.

Miriam Drennan

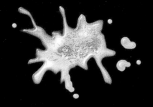

Special thanks to Abe Goolsby for his twisted thinking and great retouching skills, which made the motivational posters in each chapter so inspiring.

Also, I'd like to thank Jade Novak, Roy Roper, Jay Smith, Kristi Carter Smith, David Thomas, Darren Welch, Dawn Verner, and all the talented folks here at Anderson Thomas Design, Inc., for adding to this team effort. Thanks for putting up with me as a picky creative director, and thanks for soaring above the madness each and every day.

Miriam, thank you for not writing too many things about me in this book, or at least disguising the references to me so I'd be the last to know.

Joel Anderson

How to Use This Book

In the fast-paced, cut-throat business world, the useless have their cheesy motivational posters and the rest of us have large doses of reality.

Do these guys really think they can pacify us with high-brow generalizations? Puh-leez.

The author spent ten years carefully researching this phenomenon by conducting experiments, analyses, and pity parties. What you hold in your hands is the result: a single, easy-to-follow volume, capable of guiding millions through their workdays. Guard its wisdom well, lest it fall into the hands of a higher-up or entry-level schmoe; tell 'em to find their own how-to guides.

This reference book was created with you in mind, dear reader: the real person who actually works for a living. You know the territory—now learn how to navigate through it with our time-tested maneuverings. You'll recognize circumstances, characters, and opportunities that—when properly handled—can make the hours from 8 to 5 seem more like 8 to 4:30.

By the way, use our suggestions at your own risk. If you learn nothing else after studying this book, learn not to take it all so seriously.

TEAMWORK

All for one, and one for all—
so long as that one is not you.

TEAMWORK

Keep the End Result in Sight

It is important to understand the true value of teamwork, particularly in office situations. Pepper your conversations with words and phrases promoting the teamwork concept—the more clichéd, the better. A starter list:

"All for one, one for all."
"Rome wasn't built in a day."
"This is a group effort."
"We're a family here."
"There is no 'I' in teamwork."

A true professional knows how to give teamwork continual lip service while keeping a mental tally of those who drop the ball, have bigger offices, and arrive late. Even team players have their limits, right?

Word of caution: Don't become so proficient that you buy into your own teamwork hype.

Teamwork has its benefits, too, particularly when office rhetoric comes into play. For example, say the boss asks, "Who made the mess in the kitchen?" No one should respond. Or say the project manager asks, "Who is responsible for this typo?" No one should look up from his/her computer. Other rhetorical questions overheard in the office:

"Who forgot to turn off the coffee pot?"
"Who was responsible for sending this package?"
"Who broke the copier?"
"Who knows how to boot the server?"
"Why does the supply closet have that funny smell?"

With no admission of guilt or knowledge, no one person gets stuck with the mess. Remember, you're all in this together.

The team that works together stinks together.

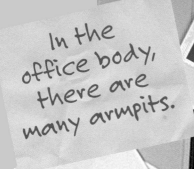

In the office body, there are many armpits.

Your office encourages too much togetherness when...

1. You carry pictures of one another in your wallets.
2. Bathroom breaks require the buddy system.
3. You hold hands during your performance review.
4. Staff field trips include grocery bulk-buying trips to discount warehouse clubs.
5. The office retreat must count as vacation time.
6. Your staff meeting agenda includes a notation for "Emotional Cleansing."
7. Your boss asks, "Whose week is it to host the Friday Night Sleepover?"
8. Your boss insists on everyone calling him/her "Pookie."
9. Your company's slogan is "It's a Group Thing."
10. You qualify as a common-law marriage.

Dr. Happy, licensed
lobotomist
1-800-LOBOT-ME

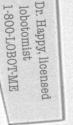

Hi-Ho Smiley-Schmooze, Office Cheerleader

Common titles: Administrative Manager, Office Assistant, Internal Correspondence Associate, Resource Management

Identified by: Happy ambiguous memos that, when deciphered, usually amount to a bit of misery for the recipients. Example:

> Hi-Ho, all!
> Everyone is encouraged to turn out early Saturday morning—our own boss will be running in the January Jaunt! As a mark of support, we're asking everyone to wear running shorts and a tank top—what's a little chill, after all, when it's for a good cause? The run starts at 5:30 A.M. at the downtown mall—get there early, 'cause parking's at a premium and we want to take a group photo!

In other words, you're expected to rise with the chickens on your day off and wear skimpies in cold weather—not to mention the fact that there will be photographic evidence of your absence if you try to skip it.

Worst trait: The self-proclaimed eyes and ears of the big guns, totally contradicting the whole "team-player" mantra.

Best trait: Easily flattered, easily flustered. Using obvious melodrama, tell Hi-Ho that you don't know what your office would *do* without him/her. Lay it on thick! Hi-Ho is so self-centered he/she won't realize you're making fun until it's too late. And the beauty of this approach is that there is no way Hi-Ho can repeat this to the boss without sounding like he/she can't take a compliment—and how out of character would that be? Hi-Ho virtually grovels for compliments.

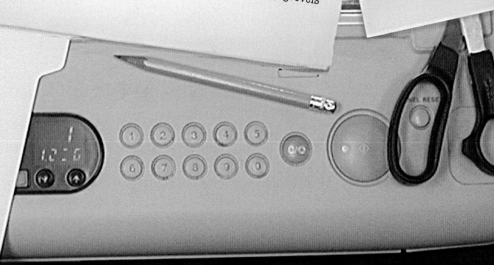

Rate Yourself:

What kind of teamplayer are you?

1. Your supervisor has been picking on you all week, claiming you don't work fast enough and don't show enough follow-through. Just before quitting time, she is hit with a deadline of 8:00 the following morning and tearfully asks if you could work late. You:

a. Smile sweetly and say, "Of course I'll stay. But I will need five minutes to rearrange some things." Well, okay, you didn't have plans to "rearrange," but her guilt could mean big things for you.

b. Kind of snicker and say, "Sorry, I have plans I can't change—I'm seeing a show." Well, okay, so the show is *Friends*—but how likely is NBC to change its programming to accommodate your working late?

c. Clear your throat and say, "First, please remind me—what was it you were saying about my speed and accuracy?" Groveling is a beautiful thing—so long as you're not the one doing it.

d. Agree to stay late to work, but secretly plan to go through the HR files to get blackmail scoop.

2. Carl has been the mail clerk for three months, yet his incompetence remains unchecked. Carl, on the other hand, thinks he's ready to be a big shot in the sales division. When a very important client fails to receive a very important package, your supervisor wants to know why. You:

a. Take it on the chin. You're feeling generous—Carl is in your charge, technically.

b. Suggest to your supervisor that Carl be promoted immediately to sales.

c. Don't say a word—just point to Carl.

d. Respond with, "I've been trying to work with him on these issues. Since he's my responsibility, I guess it's ultimately my fault." Your boss won't hear this last part—she's too busy exploding in front of Carl.

3. You go to the copier and discover a confidential memo about layoffs has been left inside. What do you do?

a. Quietly return it to the president and say, "This will remain confidential."

b. Post it on the billboard in the break room with a yellow stickie that says, "This was left in the copier. Does it belong to you?"

c. Strut around the office, dropping enough hints to let folks know that you know something is up, but not dropping enough hints to get in trouble for letting the cat outta the bag.

d. Strike a deal with the higher-ups: They want their memo? Then you keep your job. It's that simple.

4. A coworker suggests a departmental slow-down that would get the boss's attention. You respond by:

a. Tipping off the boss in hopes that you keep your job.

b. Kicking yourself that you hadn't thought of the idea yourself.

c. Telling him it's a bad idea, that perhaps if the department showed a profit, everyone could keep their jobs.

d. Organizing the whole thing yourself and calling it a "crawl along" so you can claim the idea as your own and your department will think you're cool.

SCORING:

It's pretty simple—give yourself 1 point for every "a" answer, 2 points for every "b," 3 points for each "c," 4 points for each "d."

4–6: You fluctuate between loyal and passive-aggressive behavior. If you can be rewarded for teamwork, that'd be okay, but if you can get ahead only by blowing the whistle on everyone else, then that's okay too. We would suggest you make up your mind already, but chances are, you've lived a lifetime without taking a stand—why change now?

7–9: You've all but given up—or to put it in a positive spin, you have mostly accepted—your work situation. At this point, your job is pretty much one big game of aggravation, whether you're giving or receiving. Your team consists solely of you.

10–12: With you, it's all about the show. And pointing the finger of blame. Either way, accept that you have no friends at work.

13–16: Not only have you accepted your work situation, you also know how to work the system. You know just how valuable teamwork is to the office, and you're not about to give anymore than the absolute minimum. Keep up the good work, you so-called teamplayer!

Team-Building Idea:
Does your boss overuse a certain word or phrase? Before your next staff meeting, create an office pool among your coworkers to determine how many times they think the boss will use his trademark phrase or word. Winner gets a free lunch using money taken from either the stamp fund or petty cash.

Nugget O'Wisdom:
Strike while your employer has a big contract. —Ambrose Bierce

From the *Glossary of Professional Terms:*
Pavlovian: *adj.* Office term used to describe those who perform only when their supervisor enters their cubicle. Generally dislikes teamwork, often uses the phrase, "That's not in my job description."

Example: *Studies have proven that Pavlovian employees also respond if life-size cardboard cut-outs of their bosses are left at the entrance of their cubicles; this saves supervisors a tremendous amount of time, especially when patrolling offices.*

Daytime Trauma:
If your office is like a soap opera, consider these nicknames:

* The Young and the Useless
* One Life to Give
* Search for the Internet
* All My Chidin'
* As the Rolodex Turns
* General Hostility
* Another World Altogether
* Days of Our Spies
* Fluorescent Light

United we seem,
divided we are.

One dark and stormy night...

an elderly farmer in a quaint village was attempting to corral his livestock. As the winds whipped through his tiny farm, he called to his small herd of cattle and sheep. His prized horse broke away and galloped through the tiny village, alerting the people that trouble was brewing.

The villagers tore from their beds and raced to the farm to assess the situation. "We haven't much time," said one of the villagers. "Every second counts. Everyone must cooperate!"

The elements against them, they quickly devised a plan of action that would make the most of their dwindling time. Banding together against torrential rain and gusting wind, they pilfered as many sheep and cows as they could. Winter was coming, so they needed all the wool and milk they could get their hands on.

Teamwork—it takes a village.

SERVICE

*Make 'em wish they'd
done it themselves.*

SERVICE

A Mentoring Opportunity

Service is key to workplace survival. A service-minded attitude should apply not only to the business/customer relationship; the coworker/coworker relationship must be considered as well. Adopting a mind-set of service can make the most demeaning of tasks bearable. What one must do, however, is delegate these tasks to someone who's clueless.

Office interns and wimpy new hires desperately need this kind of opportunity. Don't shy away from your responsibilities as a seasoned player—you owe it to them to teach the value of service-mindedness. Grunt work, in particular, teaches humility, reinforces various skills, and creates an adherence to deadlines.

Drafting your correspondence, filing, screening your calls, cooking your dinner, picking up your laundry or children—these are all tasks that provide a valuable service. Sure, the valuable service benefits *you*, but how else do you prepare these young doofuses for the future? You would perform a *disservice* by not giving the clueless these sorts of opportunities!

And what do you do with those employees who actually complete their assignments? Easy—call for a do-over. Repetition is a wonderful brain-sharpening mechanism—and it keeps their eye-rolling skills in top-notch condition!

What they don't know won't hurt them—and if they don't know their job description, that's to your advantage. If they give you any guff, simply say, "We must remember that we are here to perform a service. I would never ask you to do anything that I am unwilling to do myself."

Hey, if you'd been willing to do the task, you would have never delegated it in the first place. But that's not the point—the point is, an attitude of service is key to workplace survival. Survival of the cleverest, that is.

A *simple smile* can *cover up* a *wealth of incompetence.*

Knifenbacker, Passive-Aggressive Player

Common titles: Shipping Manager, Assistant to Accounts, Boss's kid

Identified by: A never-ending supply of rocks and hard places. Two faces. Usually has a nice collection of legs taken from others so that they will have nothing to stand on. Knifenbacker is the least helpful person in the office, and one of the most bitter. He/she feels very put-upon and underappreciated, even though his/her sole purpose is to make others miserable in such a way that the finger of blame can't be pointed back at him/her.

Knifenbacker is usually responsible for all the mail and shipping, too, which amounts to your having to run to the post office yourself after missing his/her arbitrary shipping deadlines. Don't despair, though, Knifenbacker keeps a map in the desk drawer so you won't have to call for directions. It's the Knifenbacker way of being helpful.

Best trait: Knifenbacker is fair and treats everyone this way.
Worst trait: Selective hearing.

A wagging tongue and a dull mind are usually found in the same head.

The proverb warns that "you should not bite the hand that feeds you." But maybe you should, if it prevents you from feeding yourself.

Thomas S. Szasz

One good thing about being wrong is the joy that it brings to others.

Start each day with a smile— and get it over with.

–W.C. Fields

REQUIRED OF ALL EMPLOYEES

Wayst O'Time Seminars Presents:

YOUR STAPLER & YOU

THIS FRIDAY, 5:00 P.M. UNTIL ?????

Millions suffer from stapler abuse, but are too ashamed to admit it. It is estimated that each day, 4.5 million people worldwide receive some type of injury resulting from a stapler. If you are one of those people, you are not alone.

But take heart—it doesn't have to be this way.

Join us for an in-depth look at stapler dysfunction; learn the early warning signs of stapler insubordination. Learn about staple removers that can offer a fresh start.

You can have a healthy relationship with your stapler— it's never too late.

WILL RETURN

ish

Helpful Service Hints:

A how-to guide written by seasoned veterans in the service field

If the customer ...	You respond by ...
Sighs heavily in your direction	Doing what you're doing and ignoring him.
Clears his throat for your attention	Being really focused on your inner self at the moment.
Says, "Excuse me ... "	Gritting your teeth and saying, "I'm trying to."
Asks to see the manager	Stating, "I'm the manager."
Complains to the manager	Playing dumb. Playing very dumb.
Wants to pay with anything other than exact change	Explaining, "This is an exact change register. The person who handles checks, credit cards, and making change will not be here until tomorrow."
Needs to speak directly to the billing department	Transferring him immediately to technical support.
Wonders if you might have a different size/color	Saying, "Absolutely not. I just checked, oddly enough, on that very item and all we have is what you see."
Calls on the telephone	Putting him on hold for all duration.

Hard work never hurt anyone—
but why take any chances?

From the *Glossary of Professional Terms:*
Encourage: *v.* passive-aggressive form of threat. To *strongly encourage* indicates your employment and/or health is at stake if you do not comply with the request.

Example: *Mary* **strongly encouraged** *her new assistant Jack to take her cat to its nail salon appointment in an effort to cultivate his service-mindedness and team-playing skills.*

One dark and stormy night...

an elderly farmer in a quaint village was walking toward town to purchase a wool sweater and some milk. He'd recently lost his sheep and cows, forcing him to purchase this kind of stuff. Coincidentally, a store had just opened nearby that featured these two very items, so he counted himself fortunate that he would not have to do without during the winter months.

He entered the store (which had a funny smell), and his eyes were drawn immediately to a soft black sweater. A lump rose in his throat and his hands delicately patted the garment as he remembered his favorite sheep whose wool was almost identical to the wool in the sweater. He recalled fond moments spent chasing her, feeding her, shearing her, singing to her, playing cards with her. All the little things he did for her added up to one thing: service through love. He smiled as his mind drifted to another place, another time. Tears began to well in the elderly farmer's eyes, but it's possible that the funny smell was the cause, not fond memories.

"That'll be eighty-five dollars. And hurry it up, we're closing," said the salesperson, hiding her face lest she be recognized as one of the villagers from that other dark and stormy night in the previous story.

Service—some get it, some don't.

ACHIEVEMENT

When your moment of supreme triumph finally arrives, relish it for all it's worth. It won't last.

ACHIEVEMENT

Because You Have an Inflated Sense of Entitlement

Achievement involves setting not just professional goals, but personal goals as well. Through hard work, determination, perseverance, setting your own goals and standards—and not competing with others—one can achieve great things. There's no reward quite like personal satisfaction.

Unless, of course, you can get there quicker by bypassing all that mumbo-jumbo and reap those rewards sooner rather than later.

And what is, exactly, the reward for all your effort? Why, vacation of course! By golly, you've earned it—so what if no one else thinks so? We've already stated that achievement is not about competing with others.

We understand that everyone cannot afford to take "official" time off—much less leave town for a bona fide vacation. Everyone, however, can take an office vacation! Remember, *you've earned it.*

It may be as simple as hanging out in the break room or copy room for several hours or as elaborate as installing tanning bulbs in your desk lamp. Once you've designated an official "I Am Not Working Today" day, how you choose to spend your in-house vacation is entirely up to you. Run a fan and a space heater simultaneously to create a tropical breeze. Put one of those little umbrellas in your coffee or water cup. Take a slow, personal tour of your office building in the morning—and bring a camera for snapshots (claim that the pictures will go in the office photo album, even though you're really updating your dartboard collection). Wear your swimsuit under your clothes and catch a few rays in the early afternoon. Don't answer the phone or be helpful—after all, you're on vacation!

As with any vacation, however, in-house vacations require their own travel insurance: download a free spreadsheet to give the illusion that you're doing something that's complicated and requires numbers. Achievement has its rewards, indeed, but there's no sense in setting yourself up for a permanent vacation or anything. Safety always comes first.

In-house vacations: No agent. No bills. No work.

In-House Vacations

Ready for a vacation but uncertain of your destination? There is rest for the weary—check out these possibilities!

Top In-House Vacation Sites:

1. Boss's office (barely used, luxury furnishings, nice view)
2. Parking lot (breezy, places to hike, ground transportation available)
3. Elevator (the "amusement park" ride every in-house vacationer must experience)
4. Break room (most popular with the "munch bunch," bound to see someone you know)
5. Copy room (popular place to make pictures)
6. Server room (techie haven)
7. Supply closet (good selection of souvenirs)
8. Bathroom (facilities available)
9. Conference room (remote and undisturbed—good for campers)
10. Someone else's office (timeshare of the in-house vacationing set)

MANDATORY MEETING Friday, 5:30 P.M.—????

Replacing a Pen Cap in 12 Easy Steps

Session I: Ballpoint, Felt Tip, or Ink—which is right for you? Are the re-capping steps different for each pen type?

Session II: Pull-off Cap vs. Twist-off Cap—three time-saving tricks that can save your ink. Recommended for advanced cappers.

Session III: Pencils—a thing of the past? A panel of experts from the writing utensil industry will debate this hot, hot issue.

Glory Swiper, Stealer of Thunder

Common titles: Receptionist, Clerk, Vice President, your supervisor

Identified by: Taking credit for successful projects, regardless of whether he/she had anything to do with them. Permanent in-house vacation status. Often has tendency to shun responsibility if something goes wrong. Usually rewarded with promotion or extra vacation time (the real kind, not the in-house kind).

Best trait: You can identify him/her very, very quickly.
Worst trait: The CEO can't.

to-do list:
- Watch own back
- Plan a sick day
- Get a life

23

Rate Yourself:

Achievement: how high do you aim?

1. When you think about achievement, what comes to mind is:
a. A promotion and golf three times a week.
b. A perfect three-pointer landing in your wastebasket.
c. You've finally gotten rid of Carl in shipping.
d. Your boss asks your opinion, even if it's only about the weather.

2. You are notified that a position on the next level of management has been vacated. They're considering hiring from within, but are having a difficult time deciding who deserves the promotion. You:
a. Casually remind the decision makers about the flaws of the others being considered. For example, the next time you're meeting with the vice president, say, "And speaking of quarterly earnings, remember that time Lisa left the company's cell phone at that restaurant?"
b. Work extra hard, come in extra early, and make them think you're willing to do this all the time. Suffer through until they make a final decision—it could mean a *door* in your future.
c. Suggest (within earshot of the decision makers) that you would appreciate moving upward and onward; they may be thinking that you enjoy what you're doing and would be upset to leave your coworkers behind.
d. Remember the confidential layoff memo that you found (see Rate Yourself, page 10). Calmly slide it under the boss's nose and say, "Now about that promotion..."

3. You receive the promotion, only to discover it ain't what you thought. You actually have to work! How do you walk the fine line between a demotion and a dismissal?
a. Draft a fake memo to your boss from your former coworkers, asking for you to come back to their fold.
b. Start sitting at your old desk again and pretend the promotion never happened (unless, of course, it's paycheck time).
c. Hide your phone and computer so that you can't do your job.
d. Carefully reword your former job description and adopt it as your current job description. Cut your work in half, keep the office, and now comes sofa-snooze time!

4. Which of the following best describes your career goals?

a. Make it to the office on time two mornings per week.

b. Finagle an introduction with the company's founder and charm mercilessly until you get promoted into a useless position.

c. Goals? What goals? Who said anything about goals?

d. All of the above.

SCORING:

It's pretty simple: 1 for "a" answers, 2 for "b" answers, 3 for "c" answers, 4 for "d" answers.

4–6: You have all the makings to be a planner and schemer, but your attention span is so short you don't bother thinking things through. Maybe when you grow up, things will be different.

7–9: With you, it's all schmooze and no substance. As a schmooze purist, you will live in fear and rightfully so; someone's gonna blow your cover—it's only a matter of time.

10–12: You're terrific at achieving plans and schemes. The problem is you're not very well liked. You know the saying "You don't have to like me, but you do have to work with me"? Well, unlearn it.

13–16: You're doing a good job at achieving goals—alas, hardly anyone notices. This could be advantageous, particularly if you screw up. With this in mind, some goals are definitely better than others—you'd much rather brag to your former coworkers about the three-pointer in the wastebasket than present a five-year plan to the board of directors, right?

17+: You're either lying to yourself or your addition stinks. Go back and try again.

Personal Achievement Tips

If your boss is working your fingers to the bone, you should definitely expense your next manicure.

A three-hour lunch is the in-house equivalent of a short weekend getaway.

Didn't get enough sleep? Wear dark glasses into the office and tell everyone you've been to the eye doctor. Nightie-night.

MOMENTUM

No matter how fast you run, something will catch up to you.

From the *Glossary of Professional Terms:*
Office-social: *adj.* Usually, a term used to describe a professional relationship that does not continue outside the office, but in which those involved cannot get their work done because of all the yakking that takes place during the workday.

Example: *Rick and Helen wasted a lot of time chatting in the office, but their relationship was strictly an* **office-social** *one; it's not as if they hung out together, or were real friends or anything.*

[Editor's note: This term is often confused with *office social*, which is a painfully deliberate attempt to fabricate a close family atmosphere through a specific event. Another very important distinction is that *office social*, in this case, functions as a noun instead of a hyphenated adjective.]

One dark and stormy night...

an elderly farmer in a quaint village was walking toward the wool and dairy boutique that had been making a killing since the really bad dark and stormy night when his wool and dairy farm was destroyed. "Some guys have all the luck," he muttered to himself, plodding along in the mud.

When he arrived, he discovered what amounted to a three-ring circus! Roaming spotlights, flashing lights, horns blaring—why, this wasn't his favorite little boutique at all! This was some colossal structure with a big pink sign that read "THE ALL-NITE WOOL 'n' DAY-REE."

"What sellouts," moaned the elderly farmer. "What started out as a charming concept has evolved into corporate gluttony. And the horrid smell doesn't seem to deter customers, including me. Alas, where else am I supposed to buy wool and milk?"

Selecting his wool and a small bottle of milk, he approached the counter where his items had to be electronically scanned. "That will be $275," said the saleswoman, certain that her large headpiece and microphone shielded her identity and still kept her from being recognized.

"What?!?" cried the elderly farmer. "Why, I could travel to Bermuda at that price!"

"Fine," snapped the woman. "You certainly won't need wool in Bermuda. But you're here now. Cough it up."

Handing her every cent he had, plus an IOU, the elderly farmer trudged out of the store, back into the dark and stormy night. He noticed an eerie glow that seemed to surround the store, something inexplicable and definitely not flashing neon lights.

"I work hard, stay honest and for what?" he whispered angrily. "To have my paltry Bermuda vacation fund spent at a dairy discotheque."

True achievement isn't always recognized with dollars and flashing lights. Yeah, and keep telling yourself that.

LEADERSHIP

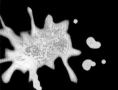

*Aspire to make the world
your personal toilet.*

LEADERSHIP

Who Holds the Keys?

Very often, we get involved in tasks so mundane that we fail to see how much one person can make a difference. You may think one person can't change the world; alas, one person can change *your* world.

So choose your one person carefully and let 'em know who's boss. Some possibilities to help you in the selection process:

- The nuisance hired into your office microcosm who thinks he's gonna "whip those incompetents" into shape.
- The person who has to hold a meeting about everything.
- The other person who yaks incessantly in all those meetings, making them last twice as long. That person's yakking so much, everything has to be repeated because he misses it the first time around.
- The person who abides by every rule and policy, and lets everyone know when you're not.
- The guy who has an opinion about everything and will offer it, unsolicited.

When dealing with your one person, remember that little things mean a lot. Here, too, we offer many options. Try ours, but don't be afraid to tap into your imagination—real leaders are nurtured by imagination! To get you started, we offer the following suggestions:

- Clip his paperclips together and return them to the dispenser; it sends the message, "Hey, buddy, be on your guard."
- Depending on your filing system, change a few labels or mix 'n' match her folders as a way of saying, "This office ain't so private, after all."
- If you really want to drive your message home, take one of her files and later ask for it—that should keep her occupied for hours.

Leadership can indeed mean the difference between a fluorescent-lighted cubicle and a corner office.

**Eagles may soar, but turkeys
don't get sucked into jet engines.**

Space Invader, Touchy-Feely Boss

Common titles: Former Shipping Manager and/or Assistant to Accounts, Chief Orchestrative Officer, the Boss's other kid

Identified by: Bleeding heart and puppy-dog eyes. Always wants to hug, especially after eating raw onions and cooked cabbage on a hot day while wearing no deodorant.

Best trait: Pushover for extra vacation days.

Worst trait: Would rather have friends than respect due to lack of attention from absentee, empire-building Daddy.

ATTENDANCE IS REQUIRED

Envelopes: Stuff About Stuffing
Friday, 5:00 P.M. until ?????

General Session: Seal the Deal
New arguments for the age-old Tongue vs. Sponge debate.

Break-out sessions:
• Sealing glues: Low-fat or cherry-flavored, find the sealing glue that's right for you.
• Assembly lines: Survival tips for mass mailings.

Joan—
-Rat poison
-Drain cleaner
  Can you tell
   the difference
     between either
       of these and,
     say, the
        powdered
          sugar on a
            doughnut?

  Just curious.
  — Martha

Leadership, Unmasked

Think your boss is crazy? At last, you can interpret the signs. Read on:

If this happens ...	It means that ...
A futon and shower are installed in the office.	Communal living is under consideration.
More and more candles are added to the office decor.	They can't pay the power bill. Start looking.
Your office is decorated in authentic "retro."	Your boss purchased a lake house and bought your office furniture at Rocko's House O'Cheap.
A memo is circulated about expenses.	Your boss can't afford the lake house.
Your boss suggests "open air" offices.	You'll find your "Rocko Special" desk on the street tomorrow.
You're signed up for kitchen duty.	You are despised among equals.
Your voicemail isn't working.	Your days are numbered.
A memo is circulated about postage expenses.	The lake house needs new curtains.
The boss flies his family to Milan for a month.	He has sold the lake house, changed his name, and will never be found. Get ready to use your last paycheck to pay off the Rocko balance, sucker.

Rate Yourself:

What kind of leader are you?

1. Congratulations—you've been put in charge of the high school intern program! What kind of screening process do you set up to determine who will be selected?

a. One that includes only the boss's kid and his spoiled friends.

b. An entrance exam that pulls from the LSAT, MCAT, or GRE.

c. No screening process, because the idea of the company being overtaken by teenagers sounds like an improvement.

d. Go global and get interns who do not speak any English whatsoever.

2. How do you rope coworkers into serving as mentors for the interns?

a. Tell them you heard a rumor about a little bonus that will be given to staff participants. But underscore that it's *just* a rumor.

b. They can mentor now, or pay later. Their choice.

c. Stoop to shallow, insincere flattery, just this once.

d. Remember that massive blackmail folder? Time to break it out, bucko.

3. You did such a good job with the high school intern program, you've been assigned the position of kitchen coordinator for the next quarter. What is your response?

a. Oh, please. That old line? You got stuck 'cause nobody else wanted to do it, just like the intern program.

b. Wear that kitchen duty badge with honor—and adapt your mentor recruitment tactics to fit your kitchen recruitment program (see question 2).

c. Initiate a second high school intern program, and get them to work in the kitchen.

d. Announce "free food in the kitchen!" and lock the door. No one's getting out till that place sparkles!

4. What is your approach to conflict resolution?

a. Buy two Louisville Sluggers.

b. Tell them all what they want to hear and then go into hiding.

c. There are no conflicts if you take on the role of dictator.

d. Three words, lotsa choices: denial, denial, denial. Head in sand. Ignore the problem. Don't pass "Go." Get out quick. Someone else's problem.

SCORING:

Okay, if you haven't picked up on this by now, we'll go over it again. It's really very simple: give yourself 1 point for every "a" answer, 2 for "b," 3 for "c," and so on and so forth.

4–6: You're the kind of leader who will buy cheesy motivational posters for your underlings, and both you and your staff know it's a big lotta hype. Still, you kinda do what you're told without thinking—very robotic, puppet-like leadership skills, which kind of defeats the purpose.

7–9: Boy, are you tough. Or at least you think you are. Get over it—you're not "all that," or whatever phrase the kids are saying these days.

10–12: You're just about there, as far as leadership skills are concerned, down to the fumbly bumbliness that gives your employees fodder.

13–16: Well, you probably passed all your psychology classes in school with flying colors. But that just means you're good at manipulation. Yeah, there's a lofty goal.

Nuggets O'Wisdom:

One tiny pebble can make hundreds of ripples in the water, but your boss would make a huge splash if you shoved him in.

The world may be your oyster, but oysters rank pretty low on the food chain.

Egos always endure ... they remain long after the backbiting is forgotten.

The thief to be most wary of is the one who steals your time.

Think you want to be the big cheese at your office? Think again.

—The Farmer in the Dell

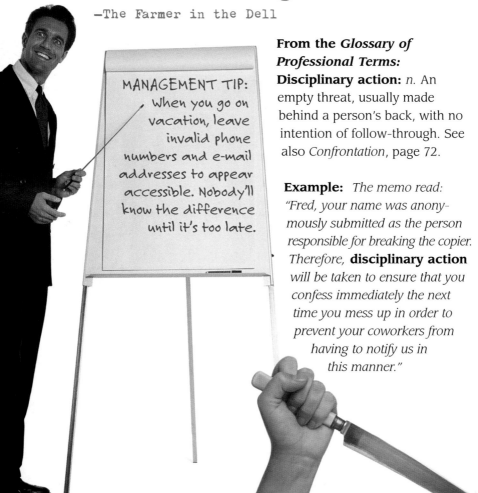

MANAGEMENT TIP: When you go on vacation, leave invalid phone numbers and e-mail addresses to appear accessible. Nobody'll know the difference until it's too late.

From the *Glossary of Professional Terms*:
Disciplinary action: *n.* An empty threat, usually made behind a person's back, with no intention of follow-through. See also *Confrontation*, page 72.

Example: *The memo read: "Fred, your name was anonymously submitted as the person responsible for breaking the copier. Therefore, **disciplinary action** will be taken to ensure that you confess immediately the next time you mess up in order to prevent your coworkers from having to notify us in this manner."*

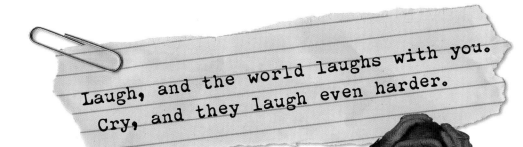

Laugh, and the world laughs with you.
Cry, and they laugh even harder.

Bacteria is often the only
culture some people have.

One dark and stormy night...

an elderly farmer in a quaint village was tired of walking into town. The prices on wool and milk were sky-high, and he thought he might get a better price at one of those discount superstores in the next city. Then he remembered his prized horse from the first chapter and thought, "Hey, whatever happened to that horse? I could ride him to the discount superstore and save myself a lot of time."

Sure enough, he found the horse nearby, yukking it up in a field with some wild horses. It was pretty obvious the horse had gotten mixed up with the wrong crowd. The farmer paid no attention to the wild horses, threw a bridle on his old horse, and rode him to the discount superstore in a neighboring town. When he pulled the reins to brake, the horse bucked him from his back.

Leadership—sometimes, it's not as simple as the distinction between a cubicle and a corner office. Sometimes it's determined by who runs wild and free and who is dropped on his posterior.

PRIORITIES

*You'll never forget what's most important
if you remember it is yourself.*

PRIORITIES

Checklist for Success

One of the most difficult (yet beneficial) things a professional can do is prioritize. Daily, weekly, monthly, and even long-term priorities make life far more manageable than living life in hit-or-miss mode.

How else will you return all your personal calls and answer e-mail? Or run a few errands? If you don't schedule these matters, they'll never get done. And if that means scheduling them between the hours of 8 A.M. and 5 P.M., well ... so be it. It all evens out in the end, anyway—if you average about three to four hours of work each day, and compute your wages based on that number, you are probably making a decent hourly wage and therefore can justify your "part-time" hours.

Well, now that's settled—so how do you spend the rest of your day?

Out of respect for your boss, determine what can be done during hours that reasonably correspond with his schedule. Phone calls can be made during those early morning "settling in" minutes. Internet browsing/purchasing and small errands can be accomplished during your boss's lunch hour (certainly not during *yours*). Schedule errands and matters that require larger pockets of time—Christmas shopping, workout, golf, midday naps—during those times your boss has "special" lunches that require him to leave at a specific time and will keep him off the premises for a few hours. Leave five minutes after you're certain he's gone; he'll never know exactly when you left and you're as free as a bird for the rest of the afternoon.

And should your boss take a day off, you've pretty much received a free day yourself. Sleep in, take a long lunch, leave early—but carry a clipboard or something and act as if it's all "official" to deflect attention. When your boss returns, don't forget to tell him how much he deserved his day off; there's no need to mention how much you deserved his day off, too.

Yes, prioritizing your day in this manner relieves a great deal of unnecessary stress and opens the door to a more fruitful life.

Do unto others before they do unto you.

Foodie, the Office Refrigerator

Common titles: Chief Clerk in Charge of Filing and Resources, Facilities Administrator, Employee Relations Technician

Identified by: Being first on the scene when someone calls, "Food in the kitchen!" Foodie operates on a "first come, first to eat it all and save some for no one" basis. Say a client, for example, sends the office a box of chocolates—Foodie's the one who pokes his/her fingers in all the chocolates and leaves all the ones with the pink filling. Eventually, Foodie will return, however, try the ones with the pink filling, eat them all, and decide that he/she still doesn't like them. It doesn't matter what's offered—cookies, tacos, ketchup, or raw beets—if it's free and it's food, Foodie's there.

Best trait: Will eat any and all leftovers, no matter how long their shelf life.
Worst trait: Tends to suck up to von Stupid*, thinking that doing so will deliver a free lunch or two.

*For more information about Thickwit von Stupid, see page 51.

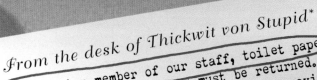

From the desk of Thickwit von Stupid*

As a senior member of our staff, toilet paper
that is borrowed and used must be returned.
Please be advised that toilet paper provi-
sionaries is a wonderful benefit our company
provides—let's not take advantageous of it.
Your cooperation is found to be appreciated
from all of the uppermost managerialistic
positions.

*oh, that's just great – I didn't know that
toilet paper had been promoted to senior staff!*

How to Prioritize Your Day:

Tomorrow morning when you arrive at the office, do nothing until you decide the order in which you will accomplish each task. Take your time and don't rush things. Your list may look something like this:

1. Phone Mother.
2. Surf the Internet.
3. Make long-distance calls to Craig, Su-Su, and Irma.
4. Peruse latest AnnTaylor or J. Crew catalog.
5. Surf the AnnTaylor or J. Crew websites to see if there are better prices online.
6. Email Craig, Su-Su, and Irma to see if there's anything fun and exciting to do where they live this weekend.
7. Order AnnTaylor and J. Crew stuff.
8. Call Craig, Su-Su, and Irma to let them know about purchases.
9. Lunch (which begins when food has actually been served).
10. Check eBay for the latest auctions.
11. see #10.
12. see #10.
13. Shuffle papers when boss walks by to convey the message, "Hey, I'm busy."
14. Pick up the phone and pretend to discuss business.
15. Repeat steps 10–15 for the remainder of the afternoon.

A ringing phone is SOMEONE ELSE'S priority.

Nugget O'Wisdom:
Feather your own nest while
others around you are molting.

From the *Glossary* of *Professional Terms*:
Challenge: *n.* Pollyanna word meaning problem that you're stuck with.

Example: *Stan's boss told him: "Your* **challenge** *is to arrange a meeting for twenty-five people," when in fact the real "challenge" was the appropriated budget, which wouldn't buy a sack of dog food.*

One dark and stormy night...

an elderly farmer in a quaint village discovered he was near poverty. His prized horse was staying out late with a wild crowd, and his sheep and cows—which had disappeared several weeks ago—never returned. Opening his last can of beans, he decided to map out a plan of action, prioritizing his steps. He made a list:

1. Find sheep and cows.
2. Tell horse he's grounded without television privileges.
3. Resume dairy and wool farming.
4. Prosper.

Then the farmer went to bed—he wanted plenty of rest before his big day. He tossed and turned, bothered by a flashing glow. The wool and dairy shop's neon sign shone brightly for miles; even when it was turned off, there was an eerie glow surrounding the shop that could be seen at all hours. All night, people arrived from faraway places to purchase items from the All-Nite Wool 'n' Day-ree— despite the smell, despite the noise, the "All-Nite" was the "it" place for wool and dairy hipsters.

"Their power bill's likely to cost a small fortune," muttered the farmer, rising from his bed. Reaching for his list, he scratched out what he'd written and wrote instead: "Tomorrow—apply for greeter's position at discount superstore."

Prioritizing takes you one step closer to your goal.

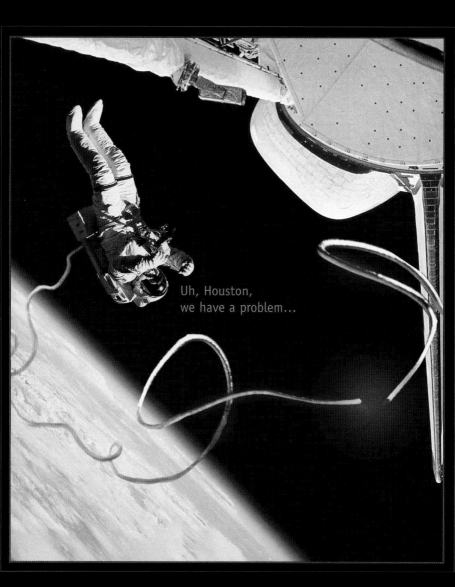

FREEDOM

Reach Your Potential Through Freedom of Choice

Freedom to do what you want, particularly in the workplace, is essential for good mental health. There are those times, however, when exercising your freedom must extend beyond the cubicle confines; this is what's known as a "sick day."

Sick days are generally reserved for times when your in-house vacations aren't cutting it, but your mental anguish isn't enough to justify taking an actual vacation day. If you elect to "be sick," however, you must also be smart, lest you fall prey to some Knifenbacker calling you, claiming he/she wants to "check" on you (when in fact, he/she just wants to nail you by telling the boss, "Well, he must be feeling better, he's not home!").

Careful planning can prevent any leaks in your sick day. Late in the afternoon on the day prior, quietly mention some nondescript symptom—sore throat, or you "just don't feel well." Very early the next morning, make an uncall* to your boss at least one hour before he/she is expected in the office and leave a message. Make sure your voice is low and scratchy—some people throw in a nasally, cold-like voice for good measure, but we don't recommend this unless you have rehearsed until it's flawless. Using a cold-like voice could also risk a Knifenbacker showing up at lunchtime with chicken soup ("Well, he must be feeling better, he's not home!").

Remember to stay on the opposite side of town or, if you are using the sick day to take a long weekend trip, make sure (in your uncall) that you have told the boss you've made an appointment to see the doctor. That way, if Knifenbacker tries to pull the usual ("Well, he must be feeling better, he's not home!"), your boss's assumption will be that you were at your appointment. Score: 1 for you, 0 for Knifenbacker.

*Glossary term, page 81.

Freedom—some days it just ain't worth gnawing through the straps.

Dr. Happy's

Excused Absences

"We'll call in sick

for you!"

1-555-FAK-EDOC

Things to Do on a Sick Day:

- Matinees (less expensive, too!)
- Catch up on reruns of *The Cosby Show* and *Designing Women* that you didn't see during the 1980s.
- Three words: Shop. Shop. Shop.
- Three more words: Sleep. Sleep. Sleep.
- Dress up in your best casual and go to a hoppin' lunch joint. Pretend you're one of those people who doesn't have to work, the kind that could spend all day there and never flinch.
- Nail salon—and do the pedicure and manicure all at once, like when Dorothy is getting cleaned up in the movie *The Wizard of Oz*.
- Check your messages. **Very** important. (Remember, Knifenbacker is hot on your trail.)

Things to Avoid on a Sick Day:

- Yard work or gardening. (You never know when Knifenbacker may do a drive-by.)
- Hair salon—a new haircut or highlights will give you away in a second.
- Three words: Your office's neighborhood.
- Calling in to "check" on things throughout the day (too suspicious).
- Hoppin' lunch joint that is frequented by your boss.
- Nail salon, if Knifenbacker is due to have claws sharpened.
- Golf, fishing, or sunbathing—a good tan will stick out in an office of pasty faces.

Freespirit Kookamongus, the Office Granola

Common title: Office Assistant (if age thirty and under);
Vice President of Controls (if age forty-five and up)

Identified by: Kooky, filmy clothes with layers of either linen or
burlap, depending on the season. Strong, musty smell with a faint hint
of incense. Appears unkempt, unbathed—usually pasty, oily face. Living
arrangements are mysterious and change frequently.

Best trait: If older, the Kookamongus knows something about what the
boss was doing at that commune several years back—and chances are,
Kook was a part of it, too. It doesn't take a genius to see the connec-
tion—and Kook's cushy office.

Worst trait: If younger, the Kookamongus spouts a bunch of high-
falutin' ideals that the rest of the world should live by; actually,
Kook's ideals get a lot of lip service, but very little court action.
Young Kook usually evolves into an annoying bunch of –isms that
drive the rest of the office to secretly boycott Joan Baez songs
and anything containing granola. Be forewarned: many Kooks
are actually hybrids of Kooks/Knifenbackers. The gentler
and more free-loving they appear, the more suspicious you
should be.

Some people leave a mark on you;
others just leave a stain.

45

> You may go the extra mile,
> but the boss will find you
> and bring you back.

Nuggets O'Wisdom

Hippocrates said, "Desperate cases need the most desperate remedies." (Helps ease the guilt of all those sick days taken, doesn't it?)

Word of caution: Munching gumdrops while walking to the fax machine does *not* replace eating fresh fruit and walking an hour during lunch.

A good rule of thumb: If it's marked "ASAP" or "immediately," it's needed in two weeks and won't get looked at for another month. Revisions will be requested approximately one hour before the big presentation takes place, however.

GET BACK TO WORK SEMINARS

———— P R E S E N T S ————

"Sick Days Are for Wimps"

BREAK-OUT SESSIONS:
- **Conference table tracheotomies:** *Making a shunt from a ball-point pen*
- **You, too, can set your own broken bones**
- **Carpal tunnel: A sissy's myth**

Save your company $$$ by performing these medical procedures on your coworkers—and get those weaklings back on task!!!!

From the *Glossary of Professional Terms:*

Surrogate Saturday: *n.* What to tell your friends when they've called you at the office and are told you're out sick and they call you to find out the truth.

Example:

Angela: "I called you at work, Chris, but they told me you were out sick today."
Chris: "Yeah, I'm taking a **Surrogate Saturday.**"
Angela: "Well, the least you could have done was told me. I could've taken one too, and we could have done something fun!"

One dark and stormy night...

an elderly farmer in a quaint village wasn't sure he felt well enough to go to his greeter job interview at a discount superstore in a nearby town. He was scheduled to talk to the manager early the next morning, and he had a tummyache from drinking some slightly curdled milk that had been on sale at the All-Nite Wool 'n' Day-ree.

When he phoned to reschedule, the manager told him that either he kept his appointment or lost the opportunity. He accused the elderly farmer of being lazy and weak willed.

"Just because you're in line for a swanky greeter position doesn't mean that you have the freedom to act like a diva!" bellowed the manager. By the time the elderly farmer hung up, he felt even sicker. That manager must be very important if he couldn't reschedule the elderly farmer's interview.

The following morning, he rose early to discover his prized horse snoring on the sofa. "Out all night again, I see," he muttered, gnashing his teeth at the thought of those wild horses. "Guess I'll have to walk."

Each mile he trod brought him more nausea. Finally, he arrived at the discount superstore drenched in sweat and with a tummy that was doing tidal waves. When the manager came out to greet him, he offered him a health drink—consisting of toothpaste and raw eggs—and it was all over. All over the manager, that is.

The lesson to be learned from this: There are times you can't control that technicolor yawn—and if your boss does not give you the freedom to choose whether you take a sick day or not, then it's on him. Literally.

COMMUNICATION

In case you were babbling under the misconception that someone is actually listening…

COMMUNICATION

Unlock the Mystery

When it comes to communication in the work environment, there is a right way to do it, and then there's a wrong way.

Osmosis and telepathy are the most commonly practiced communication methods in today's workplaces. New policies, changes in benefits/job descriptions, or nixed ideas are usually communicated through osmosis. While this is not the preferred method for the recipients, consider, for a moment, the environmental benefits: By expecting employees to gain unspoken or unwritten knowledge through absorption or fusion, supervisors do not risk polluting the air with halitosis; nor do they create a paper trail, which saves a few trees.

Changes in task or method, however, are typically handled by telepathy. There are debates as to how long this practice has been in place: Some scholars think they've traced this method's roots back to medieval times, where legends of Merlin-esque wizards were aplenty. Others argue that telepathy is a direct descendant of the ESP craze that swept the 1970s. Either theory is difficult to prove due to poorly kept records. Surprise, surprise.

Telepathy's original intent was to wow audiences, but it has since gone horribly awry. Most contemporary supervisors believe this form of communication is taught at today's universities; therefore, they telepathically add extra responsibilities to every job description. This explains why many new employees are unaware of all that will be heaped upon them once they've signed on the dotted line.

If you find yourself unable to read your boss's mind or if your success rate is touch-and-go, a nod coupled with an "I see" will usually get him/her off your back.

And remember, in terms of confrontation and conflict, passive aggression is a vital force in today's management circles.

Speak softly and carry a big bag of excuses.

READING BETWEEN THE LINES

For your own sanity, use this quick-reference guide to understand what is going on in your own workplace. Any and all of these may be used in some form of ambiguous memo, random e-mail, or staff meeting.

WHEN THE BOSS SAYS...	IT REALLY MEANS...
I can see your point.	I'm not listening to you, but I'll say anything to get you to shut your trap.
Several of you have been...	I have planted a spy among you.
It has been brought to my attention that...	I want you to think I've planted a spy among you.
Always remember that...	I've told you dead opposite before, but I'm covering my tracks so I don't get in trouble with my boss.
It appears that...	I wish I had a spy among you, but no one likes me enough to spy.
In the unlikely event that...	Brace yourself. It's gonna happen.
I will need to review this.	Don't hold your breath.
This will need to pass through several sets of eyes.	None of us has the guts to tell you "no."
I'll get back to you.	You'll retire before I give you a straight answer.
I would never ask you to do this...	Brace yourself. It's gonna happen.
Be mindful of our service-mindedness.	You're about to receive a bunch of grunt work that is beneath me.
Please be reminded that...	The spy can't catch anybody doing anything.
We have modified the following benefits...	You are about to become poorer and have less security.
We're excited about these changes...	We had no choice—the fat cats have nailed us to the wall.

50

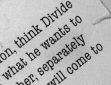

AMAZING BARNEY'S
TELEPATHIC
TRANSLATIONS
1-555-PSY-KICK

Management tip:

When it comes to conflict resolution, think Divide and Conquer: Tell one coworker what he wants to hear and do the same with the other, separately and without witnesses. Eventually, it will come to blows—but that's their problem.

PERSONAL OFFICE SUPPLY LIST:

1. Padded wallpaper
2. Ether
3. Arsenic or cyanide, whichever is on sale.

Thickwit von Stupid, Elokwent Nuisance

Common titles: Human Resources Director, Micromanager, Head Bully

Identified by: Malapropisms that he/she thinks sound intelligent and eloquent. Tendency to misspell, inflated sense of importance, has boss convinced the place would burn down if not for him/her.

Worst trait: Is given power that is undeserved and doesn't have the intellect to manage it well.

Best trait: Memos provide hours of fun, particularly for those in editorial positions.

THE COMMUNICATION HALL OF SHFAME

Great Moment in Communication History:

December 4, 1980: Congressional Record reported that the U.S. Senate's "motion to lay on the table the motion to reconsider the vote by which the motion to lay on the table the motion to proceed to the consideration of the fair housing bill (H.R. 5200) was rejected was agreed to."

...with confusion and bewilderment for all...

Open to Interpretation:

In 1697, French poet and writer Charles Perrault translated an ancient tale—more than likely originating in China—about a girl who meets her true love via her lost fur slipper. Confusing the homophones of vair and verre, old French words meaning a type of fur and glass, respectively, poor Cinderella has worn glass slippers ever since.

"[I] was provided with additional input that was radically different from the truth. I assisted in furthering that version." —Lt. Colonel Oliver North, who also used the same line as a child whenever he played "Gossip."

Spelling Test Revenge:

March 1995: Hawaiian legislature debated whether the official state fish should be the o'opu or the humuhumunukunukuapua'a.

Nugget O'Wisdom:
When in doubt, plagiarize.

The Gweat Communicatah
March 2, 1940: Elmer Fudd makes his Warner Brothers cartoon debut.

Loosely Translated?
Adolph Coors's company's slogan, "Turn it loose," was translated into Spanish and read "Suffer from diarrhea."

¿¡¿Que hablas?!?

From the *Glossary of Professional Terms:*
We: *n.* Derived from the Victorian era, used by supervisors to give the illusion of teamwork when in fact it actually refers to you and you alone, sucker.

Example: *"We have to file forty years' worth of weather reports," said Millie's boss.* Translation: *"Millie, you're on your own with this filing thing," said Millie's boss.*

One dark and stormy night...
an elderly farmer in a quaint village was waiting to hear about a job for which he'd applied at a discount superstore in a nearby town. Finally, he could stand it no longer—he had to know if they were planning to make him an offer.

He hopped on his prized horse and commanded "Hiyah!" Clicking his heels into the flanks of his prized horse, the farmer anticipated arriving at the discount superstore just prior to closing. Instead—you guessed it—the horse threw the farmer from his back and the wild horses he'd been running with tittered in amusement.

What does this have to do with communication? Exactly.

RISK

**Because you're cocky enough
to think it will work.**

RISK

The old saying, "nothing ventured, nothing gained" is actually quite true. Taking a risk on the job every now and then shows initiative and enthusiasm. Just don't get caught.

Create your own personal time zone. This requires programming at least two clocks in your office in order to arrive late, leave early, and still move ahead. Use a little common sense when adjusting the clocks to accommodate your schedule: don't program them for exactly five or ten minutes fast/slow. Instead, keep a less obvious number of minutes in mind—say, seven—when adjusting. Do not exceed thirteen minutes either way. And make sure you adjust at least two clocks—the more clocks synchronized to your personal "time zone," the better.

Save time by shopping in the supply closet. You're doing your company a favor, saving them from a huge surplus of pens, calculators, toilet paper, and anything else you can pilfer. Your coworkers may not understand the economic benefit of your shopping, so it might be best to stow these items in large briefcases, handbags, or under your coat until you're safely out of the building.

Take a healthy step forward by bringing any and all water containers to work and fill 'em up! More than likely, the fancy filters in the office coolers are far better than the lousy one at home that you'd purchased from that pyramid-scam company. And your company desires optimum health for all its employees, right? So what are you waiting for—grab a jug, and go for the gusto!

And again—we cannot stress enough how important it is to invest in a good, fake spreadsheet program. Even those in editorial positions have told us how helpful these can be when one is surfing on the Internet, e-mailing friends, and so on—one-touch access and *presto!* your hide is safe.

Risk takers savor the taste of life while the rest of us make do with a big plate o'leftovers.

How to avoid potential pitfalls when conducting risky business:

- Don't appear obvious. These are covert operations, not feats of 'cool' to impress your less-clever coworkers—this is not high school, who cares what they think?

- Don't take anything from the supply closet that has less than five remaining. Most people are too lazy to count past five, so if they glance and see plenty of calculators, for example, no one will miss one or two. But if there are four calculators, leave them alone until the next shipment arrives.

- Don't dial personal long-distance calls on a speaker phone—any Knifenbacker within earshot will hear you dialing more than seven digits. It's too suspicious—take time to lift the receiver from its cradle, and learn how to dial with your fingers barely moving across the keypad (just in case Knifenbacker has a good pair of eyes, too).

- If you need assistance learning how to dial with your fingers barely moving, consult just about any movie from the 1930s that has gangsters, newspaper reporters, or both. If a movie character picks up the phone and says something like, "Get me the commissioner!" without dialing *anything*, please know that this will *not* work on your phone: dialing is a not an option, it's a requirement.

- Don't pay your personal bills right under your boss's nose. Show a little respect by doing them behind his back, just like everyone else.

- Put *some* change in the stamp fund. Novices will just steal stamps—seasoned veterans know that you are less likely to get caught taking company stamps if you simply purchase them at a severe discount. No one will question this, so long as they hear change clanging into the box. Nickels and pennies make a loud clang, so make it count!

- It is not wise to steal food. Ever. You don't know where that stuff has been or how long it's been there. Yuck.

- Don't use your boss's well-connected name when trying to snag a table at one of his/her favorite restaurants. Instead, use it to snag a table somewhere he/she is not as likely to frequent.

Fools rush in—and take all the good seats.

Eat one live rodent first thing in the morning and nothing worse will happen to you the rest of the day.

Office Mama, aka "Marshmallow" (if male)

Common titles: Receptionist, Bookkeeping Assistant, Human Resources Associate

Identified by: Glasses sitting low on nose and frumpy dress code. Sensible shoes and dated hairstyle. Favorite saying: "How about a hug?" It's a sad commentary, particularly if the person is quite young. Has no intentions of moving anywhere else on the corporate ladder. Comes in, does job, leaves promptly—and gets away with it. Use the word "risk," and watch him/her chuckle with secretive wisdom.

Best trait: Well, okay, every now and then, a hug's not so bad.

Worst trait: When he/she gets a paper cut, sugar oozes out. Calls the boss "sugar plum" or "lamb-lamb" on the telephone. Look out: Office Mama could snap any day, without warning.

57

Nugget O'Wisdom:
Fly into the face of danger—
but watch out for the ripe acne.

More Nuggets O'Wisdom:

Don't be discouraged by the office pecking order; take comfort in the knowledge that the fattest birds are always selected first for the chopping block.

A ship in the harbor is safe... maybe that's not what ships are for, but why ruin a good paint job by taking it out to sea?

When one door closes, another opens. Seize the opportunity to stand in that little space in between the two.

A bend in the road is not the end of the road... unless it bends over a cliff or something.

A bump in the road is either an obstacle to be fought or an annoying coworker, in which case you might want to rent a steamroller for the occasion.

Don't sweat the petty things, but don't pet the sweaty things.

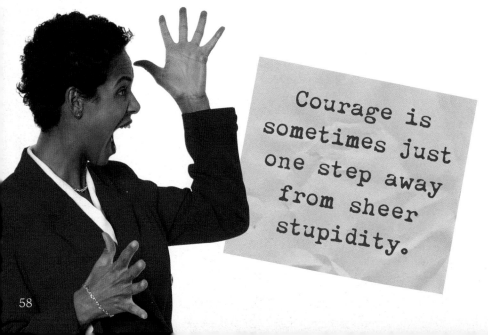

Courage is sometimes just one step away from sheer stupidity.

From the *Glossary of Professional Terms:*

Promotion: *n.* A device used by management to give subordinates more work without benefit. Usually indicated by a meaningless change in the subordinate's already meaningless current title.

Example: *Ted's* **promotion** *consists of changing his title from "Chief Flunky" to "Executive Resource Associate," but he will not receive any increase in pay.*

The growth of any organization is nurtured one schmoe at a time.

One dark and stormy night...

an elderly farmer in a quaint village arrived home from his first official day as a greeter at a discount superstore. He was weary and hungry; he planned to nibble a bit of bread and go to bed immediately thereafter.

Dragging himself up the front stairs, he envisioned a slice of bread that had never tasted so good and a downy bed that had never felt so cozy. Opening the door, he found his living room disheveled, his kitchen sink filled with water, and his dining room table covered with a big pile of hay. Not to mention his prized horse and wild friends, yukking it up to beat the band.

Yeah, it was risky for the prized horse to throw a party while the farmer was away—but the horse was really trying hard to fit in with the group.

COMPASSION

Sometimes it means putting someone out of your misery.

COMPASSION

You Know, Caring and Stuff

Compassion has a role in the workplace, just like anything else; when someone is fired, for example, show compassion by cleaning out his office—the sooner the firee cuts ties and moves on, the healthier he'll be. It's tough love, sure, but you have his best interest at heart.

Birthdays and showers are always a touchy subject—some employees will have lavish celebrations while others won't gain as much as a card. Adopt a "no party" office policy—no one is to acknowledge anyone else's special event/day during business hours. It's fair, saves the company a whopping expense, and keeps folks on the clock!

Eventually, some klutz will break both legs while skiing or something. It's expensive for your company to give him time to recuperate, so drop a few files by the hospital or his home. Bug him with phone calls, too; if you push hard enough, he may decide to cut his recuperation short— he'll have the inflated idea that the office can't survive without him.

Now, about that old dilemma of the boss's Christmas gift: the irony of purchasing a gift with a paycheck that is signed by the recipient goes beyond the scope of this book. There is an easy solution to this situation, however: enlist someone to dig something out of his/her junk closet at home. Everyone chips in a buck to cover gift-wrapping expenses, and *voila!* you have your "from the staff" gift.

A word about those times when young little future-boss is selling giftwrap, magazines, and/or cookies for the school fundraiser: If the boss is too cheap to buy enough stuff for young little future-boss to qualify for her pizza party, then what are you doing enabling her? Buying the boss a present is ironic enough, but giving the boss's kid money for cheap stuff is downright ludicrous.

Yes, when compassion is exercised in the workplace, an office saves money, time, and insurance premiums. Don't let your workplace be without it.

Have a heart...or just make it look like you do.

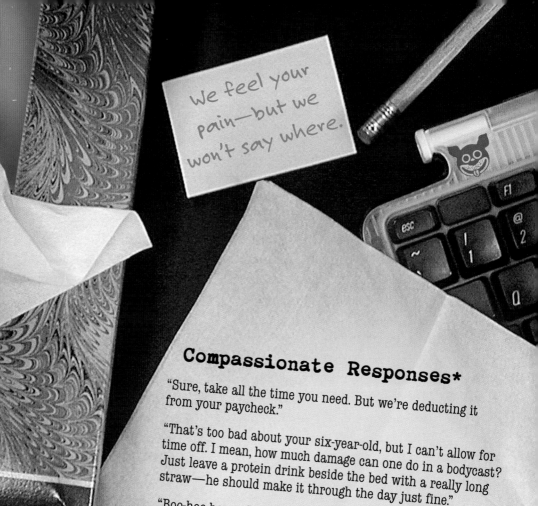

We feel your pain—but we won't say where.

Compassionate Responses*

"Sure, take all the time you need. But we're deducting it from your paycheck."

"That's too bad about your six-year-old, but I can't allow for time off. I mean, how much damage can one do in a bodycast? Just leave a protein drink beside the bed with a really long straw—he should make it through the day just fine."

"Boo-hoo-hoo... I weep for you."

"Just be glad you have a job. That oughta take your focus off those rats and cockroaches that scurry across your desk."

"Blah, blah, blah... can't you see I'm in the middle of watching *Laverne & Shirley*?"

"Don't be such a sourpuss—did your insurance plan *really* mean that much to you, or are you just mad that we're taking it away?"

"Well, try not to think about it—instead, consider the fact that you have no friends."

"I guess now wouldn't be a good time to notify you of your upcoming termination."

*compiled by retired hospital receptionists

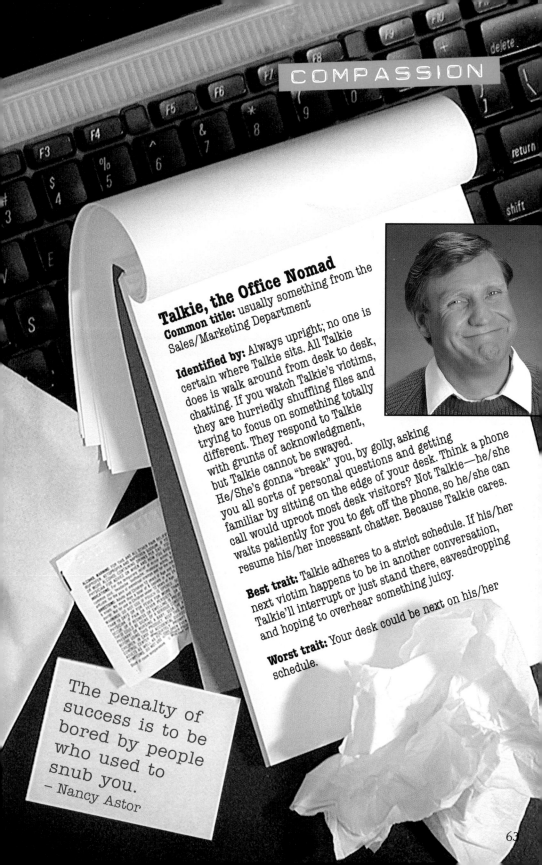

Talkie, the Office Nomad

Common title: usually something from the Sales/Marketing Department

Identified by: Always upright; no one is certain where Talkie sits. All Talkie does is walk around from desk to desk, chatting. If you watch Talkie's victims, they are hurriedly shuffling files and trying to focus on something totally different. They respond to Talkie with grunts of acknowledgment, but Talkie cannot be swayed. He/She's gonna "break" you, by golly, asking you all sorts of personal questions and getting familiar by sitting on the edge of your desk. Think a phone call would uproot most desk visitors? Not Talkie—he/she waits patiently for you to get off the phone, so he/she can resume his/her incessant chatter. Because Talkie cares.

Best trait: Talkie adheres to a strict schedule. If his/her next victim happens to be in another conversation, Talkie'll interrupt or just stand there, eavesdropping and hoping to overhear something juicy.

Worst trait: Your desk could be next on his/her schedule.

> The penalty of success is to be bored by people who used to snub you.
> – Nancy Astor

Rate Yourself:

How do you rank on compassion's scale?

1. What is your opinion of Ebenezer Scrooge?
a. The guy got a bad rap—that Bob Cratchit was nothing but an ingrate. You give Cratchit an inch, he'll take a mile.
b. Well, it all worked out in the end—why must we always focus on his bad years?
c. Scrooge, a changed man? Puh-leez. I guarantee you that by December 26, he was back to being a mean cheapskate and that Tiny Tim had to do something gross like massage his feet every night.
d. Was that the guy who was after Shemp but before Curly Joe?

2. You call into the office for last quarter's earnings reports, and your assistant accidentally deletes them from your hard drive. While he's incredibly sorry for the mistake, your boss has warned you time and again about backing up files, so this is a major boo-boo that'll cost you. What do you do?
a. Ignore it. It'll go away.
b. Scream at your assistant; tell him it's all his fault and that he will have to locate a hard copy and input the figures himself.
c. Remembering that your assistant knows just how much profit you make from your expense reports, take the problem to your boss immediately and blame it on that techie wiz who gets on everybody's nerves. Score popularity points for you, and negate popularity points for him, if that's possible.
d. Hey, isn't Agnes in Accounting responsible for keeping up with this stuff? How'd that get on your computer in the first place?!

3. Your assistant asks for a raise—she cannot pay her water bill, much less any other bill. You respond by:
a. Giving her a promotion instead. Well, not really, just a snazzier title.
b. Telling her to be glad she has a job and that only she can curtail her rock 'n' roll, extravagant lifestyle.
c. Tell her sure, okay, and then forget to turn it in to accounting.
d. Cut her salary, and see how she likes *that!*

4. Once again, someone needs time off to care for an ailing grandmother. You are overheard by eavesdroppers, and they say that you said:

a. "What is this? Did the Grandmothers' Cotillion elect to get ill this week?"

b. "There's a reason they call it 'put out to pasture.' It is a strong metaphor that you oughta consider when handling Grandma."

c. "How many grandmothers does that make this month? Hmmm?"

d. "Take as much time as you need. We have that Family Leave Act, you know. Of course, we can always come up with some other excuse to fire you. What? No, I didn't say anything. Just make sure your desk is cleaned out before you leave. What? No, I said please let your grandmother know of our grief. Enjoy this paycheck, it will be your last. What's that? No, I said I hope your grandmother recovers fast. . . ."

SCORING:

Sigh... it doesn't take a rocket scientist to figure this out.

4–6: You have all the compassion of a manager in the making. Making of what, we don't know, but your hard edge takes no favorites, especially when it comes to daily operations being upset.

7–9: You have all the tenderness of an armadillo. 'Nuff said.

10–12: You put compassion in its proper place and fly that "No Mercy" flag high and proud!

13–16: I hear tell that many industries don't require a lot of brain power. This may be a good career choice for you.

From the desk of Thickwit von Stupid:

As a senior member of our staff, it has been brought to my attention that many of you have failed in your attempts to submit provisions of funds that will be made contributable to the boss's Christmas gift. Let me remind everyone that the uppermost managerialistic executives elected to give a South American cruise, and it has demonstrated to be quite high in its expensitivity. To date, the collection contrived from the rest of the staff amounts to $10.23. Yellow stickies asking for change back have been discarded.

Therefore, I have the authorizationary requirement to declare a payroll deduction that will extracticate funds that will be earmarked for our boss's Christmas gift. This designatory draft from your paycheck will ensure that this sort of abominably atrocitytuous situation never happens again.

Nuggets O'Wisdom:

A smidge of compassion can replace a lot of pay increases.

If at first you don't succeed, blame and blame again.

If you are mediocre and you grovel, you shall succeed. —from *The Marriage of Figaro*

The stupid you always have with you. —Henry David Thoreau

All's well that pays well.

Optimists are FOOD for the JADED.

From the *Glossary of Professional Terms*:

Robinson's revenge: *n.* A project that should take only a small amount of time, but due to red tape, takes at least ten times longer. Derived from the phrase, "You'll have this finished before you can say Jack Robinson," which is often said by the supervisor when assigning said project.

Example: *"Addressing one envelope should take ten minutes max," said Nancy, "but because I had to get von Stupid's approval, it took two days. It was a definite case of* **Robinson's revenge***."*

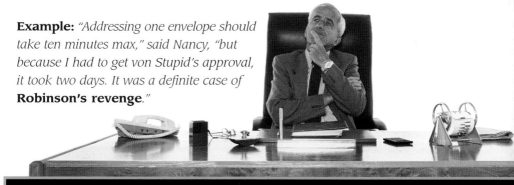

One dark and stormy night...

an elderly farmer in a quaint village had overslept after having worked the night shift at the discount superstore in a nearby city. "Oh no!" he cried, "how shall I ever make it on time?" Jerking his clothes on, he tore into the den where his prized horse had fallen asleep in front of the television. "Wake up!" he cried, "I've got to get to work, and you've got to take me! I can't be late!"

The prized horse opened one sleepy eye, rolled over on top of a half-eaten bag of pork rinds, and resumed snoring.

The elderly farmer paused to hang his head. He realized he'd been selfish—the prized horse did not have to operate on his schedule. He should have given more notice if he intended to oversleep. "Poor thing," thought the farmer. "Here he's been out all night, and just wanted to watch a bit of television to unwind from his evening antics. And then I go and disturb him." The elderly farmer felt very, very ashamed and gently covered the horse in a goosedown quilt before he tiptoed out the door.

The night manager screamed at him for his tardiness, but the elderly farmer knew that his act of compassion would probably get him in chummy with the wild horses.

RESPONSIBILITY

Why stick your neck out when you can stick your head in?

RESPONSIBILITY

A Caretaker's Heart

These days, it seems people try just about anything to get ahead—but what is wrong with trying a little old-fashioned responsibility? A whole lot, actually... unless you know how to use it.

Responsibility automatically nullifies your membership privileges as "one of the gang." No one wants to hang out with a coworker who actually works. Plain and simple.

When you are considered a responsible employee, you are setting yourself up for a lot of blame that will bubble beneath dysfunction's surface for a period of time. Be aware that the finger of blame is quietly being pointed at you, prefaced with, "Boss, I hate to tell you this since Hannah is normally a responsible employee, but I think she is the one who photocopied your face on a pig's body and taped it to everyone's desk." When enough of these allegations pile up (bubble, bubble), you can be assured that the volcano will erupt and you will get burned.

Entry levelers, interns, and part-timers are notorious for getting out of certain tasks by deliberately doing them wrong a few times. It takes only a short time for a distraught and blubbering switchboard operator, for example, to be reassigned. And guess who will be filling in until a new switchboard operator can be found? You, Mr. Responsibility Personified. And don't try pulling the same stunt as Ms. Blubbery—they'll call your bluff (and perhaps decide you're so good at handling that switchboard, you need to remain there for a while).

Responsibility also means you are willing to be held accountable for your actions... and someone else's (read: your boss). You know, like when you're given explicit instructions for carrying out a certain project, only to have your boss's boss boom, "Who did this piece of garbage?!" Guess what, yes-man? You're going down, and flying solo in the nose dive.

The good news is, by foregoing all this self-respect stuff, you can hang on to your job as chief scapegoat and patsy.

There is no need to fix the mistake
if you can fix the blame.

Blame Targets
that can never be disproven:

1. U.S. Mail
2. any delivery service
3. traffic
4. waiter
5. computer/network/server/e-mail
6. anyone who was fired recently
7. cleaning service
8. left a message
9. message not received
10. whoever's absent that day

No 9812 NAME Blackmail
NOM
July 2001

Resolve to be tender with the young, compassionate with the aged, sympathetic with the striving, and tolerant with the weak and wrong; sometime in your life they will become your boss, the way things operate around here.

Hag-a-saurus, Corporate Sacrificial Maiden
aka Sour McPrunejuice, Corporate Sacrificial Bachelor
Common title: Been there so long, no one knows

Identified by: Pinched, sour face to match pinched, sour disposition. Never has a good thing to say, never impressed by anyone or anything. Funny smell. Favorite line is, "That's not how we used to do it!" So old he/she remembers when employees were allowed to smoke at their desks. Usually owns some obscure pet—like a hamster, ant farm, or beady-eyed rat—that is spoiled rotten. Enjoys scaring young children when it's not Halloween. All new employees think they'll warm the cold beast by asking, "How are you?" and the response is always the same: "Well, I'm alive, ain't I?"

Best trait: He/she "don't get into nobody's business," and by golly, you'd better stay outta his/hers.

Worst trait: Your cube is stuck right next to his/hers.

Excuses: Instruments of thick-wits. But they sure come in handy.

Nuggets O'Wisdom:

The key to an organized desk: deeper drawers.

It is a scientifically proven fact that assistants can make themselves invisible, and they come equipped with a tracking device to prevent you from doing the same—particularly if you attempt a vacation.

Courage does not always roar. Sometimes, it is the quiet voice at the end of the day that says, "Save yourself and frame Ernie from Production for the mishap."

When a collection of brilliant minds, hearts, and talents comes together, expect to accomplish nothing. Brilliance is subjective, after all.

What lies behind us and what lies before us are tiny matters compared to what lies we're told.

Pride is a personal commitment; it is an attitude that separates the bags o'hot air from the schleps.

Never doubt that a small group of thoughtful, committed people can change the world. And if you're not a part of that group, doubt's not gonna do you much good, anyway—just ask any scapegoat.

> **After all is said and done, more is said than done.**

From the *Glossary of Professional Terms*:
Confrontation: *n.* An empty threat, usually made behind a person's back, with no intention of follow-through. See also *Disciplinary action*, page 34.

Example: *"Since he is responsible for breaking the photocopier, I am planning a **confrontation** with him," said the boss, after we'd anonymously ratted on Fred.*

One dark and stormy night...

an elderly farmer in a quaint village was thinking about his greeter job at a discount superstore in a city nearby. He was concerned about the long hours he put in each day and the tough commute he faced since his prized horse refused to carry him. "I could work better hours and get other things done if it weren't for that commute," he thought.

His employee discount from the discount superstore helped him recoup a bit of the savings he'd lost as a patron of the All-Nite Wool 'n' Day-ree. Scraping together his meager, discount superstore employee discount savings, he walked over to the All-Nite Wool 'n' Day-ree (and Now Cars, Too!) and purchased an old pickup truck that ran fairly well. He got it cheap because the truck also had that funny smell.

The truck cut his commute time in half, enabling him to work overtime or get home earlier, whichever he chose. Occasionally, the wild horses would bum a ride to somebody else's house (he didn't mind transporting them, they were big tippers). By maintaining a fiscally responsible mindset, he was able to live off the tips he was making as an underground taxi service and pocket his discount superstore paycheck.

One day, a desperate and wealthy man called on the elderly farmer's transporting services. Since the elderly farmer was running late for work, he failed to show at the prescribed hour. Later that week, the man stopped the farmer, "Hey, you!" he cried. "I missed a very important engagement because of you. How dare you call yourself a taxi service?!"

"That's just it," replied the farmer. "I don't. This whole scam got started when folks started bumming rides from me. Word definitely gets around in this town, but that doesn't mean it gets around right."

The fun thing about hearsay is that you can shun responsibility and blame the discrepancies on someone else.

PRODUCTIVITY

**Anything not worth having
is worth not working for.**

PRODUCTIVITY

Keeps Hands and Hearts Happy

When it comes to productivity in the workplace, you can take a lesson from your old driver's ed handbook: Keep with the flow of traffic.

Say you're hired at a company, and your new boss says, "I expect you to hit the ground running." If you truly hit the ground running, all that will result is more work and resentful coworkers—a deadly combination. Do not misinterpret the language of Professionalism—your boss does not want you to complete your tasks in an efficient and accurate manner. This is merely a phrase that is used to intimidate new members of the tribe.

Keep in mind that productivity is subjective—your performance review depends solely on whether your supervisor likes you. So be prepared to play along with ridiculous rules and fudge on others.

Do not work your way out of a job. Slide into the natural workflow, which usually consists of the following algebraic equation:

[deadline + (blame someone) two weeks – sleep] + [drafts x 3 (overhaul entire concept)] + three more weeks = final product

There are variations to this equation, but this is the standard from which all others derive. Deadlines will shift, drafts will multiply, but stick with this basic formula and you will not falter. It's true that a chain is only as strong as its weakest link, but it's not all red wine and roses for the strongest link, either. Strive for that nice, invisible, middle-of-the-road link status. You won't go far—but you won't be let go, either.

If you're asked for a status report while applying the equation, apply another rule of the road: Swerve and avoid. Swerve and avoid. And avoid. And avoid. After all, to quote Tom Wilson, today's greatest labor-saving device is tomorrow.

> *I never put off till tomorrow what I can possibly do... the day after.*
>
> —Oscar Wilde

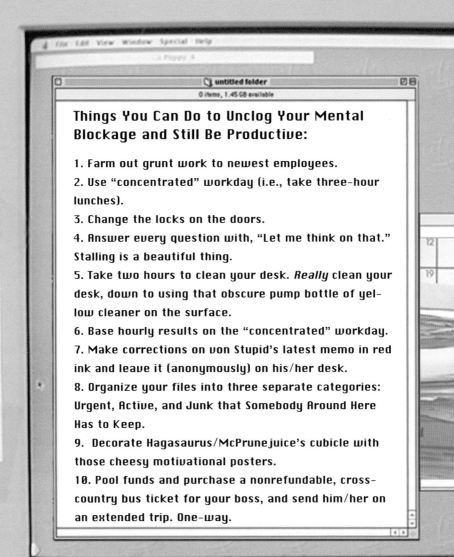

Things You Can Do to Unclog Your Mental Blockage and Still Be Productive:

1. Farm out grunt work to newest employees.
2. Use "concentrated" workday (i.e., take three-hour lunches).
3. Change the locks on the doors.
4. Answer every question with, "Let me think on that." Stalling is a beautiful thing.
5. Take two hours to clean your desk. *Really* clean your desk, down to using that obscure pump bottle of yellow cleaner on the surface.
6. Base hourly results on the "concentrated" workday.
7. Make corrections on von Stupid's latest memo in red ink and leave it (anonymously) on his/her desk.
8. Organize your files into three separate categories: Urgent, Active, and Junk that Somebody Around Here Has to Keep.
9. Decorate Hagasaurus/McPrunejuice's cubicle with those cheesy motivational posters.
10. Pool funds and purchase a nonrefundable, cross-country bus ticket for your boss, and send him/her on an extended trip. One-way.

DON'T FORGET:
Review "soul-selling" clause of employment contract!

Ever notice how the biggest complainer usually has the least amount of work to do?

Brownie, Office Kiss-up
Common titles: Coffee Pot Supervisor, Agent of Ice, Soap Dispenser Technician, Shipping Serf, Disciple of the Moment

Identified by: Power suit and inability to go to the restroom without letting the boss know. Uses phrases like "okey-dokey" and thinks the company's fax coversheets that say "Just the FAX!" are clever. Laughs at boss's jokes, always interrupts conversations because his/her business with the boss is far more important. Should boss's spouse pop by for an office visit, Brownie is practically salivating with false flattery. But you're not fooled; Brownie'll get what's coming—and it ain't the keys to the boss's beach house.

Best trait: Stylish clothes that are bought on credit.
Worst trait: Pavlovian tendencies; tends to shoot mouth off and frequently makes idiot of self.

Well-begun is half-done. Why risk the odds by finishing?

Rate Yourself:

Are you hard at work, or hardly working?

1. It's budget time, and everyone's scrambling to accomplish absolutely nothing. Your boss has asked you to itemize expenses for the entire department. Your strategy for completing this task would more than likely include:

a. Setting fire to Clara's files and pretending they're yours. You can't tabulate from files that do not exist, right?

b. Making stuff up.

c. Offering to help the techie geek with his popularity crisis in exchange for some fake spreadsheets that are so complex no one will understand them or want them explained.

d. Hopping on the Internet to see if you can buy that kind of document online.

2. You've spent the better part of a week gazing out the window and at 3 P.M. on Friday, you're handed a stack of office supply request forms to review. You consider the following options:

a. Hiding them on Thelma's desk.

b. Thinking, "At last! A fair way to conduct my paper airplane contest!"

c. Saying with a sigh, "Our confetti supply is low again already? Okay, I'll make more. Now what did I do with my scissors?"

d. Filling out one form yourself: "Toilet paper supply is low." Put the rest of the forms in the restroom to comply.

3. Where do you stand on quotas?

a. They are not a fair reflection of a person's work ethic or performance. After all, I think about actually working quite often—but you won't find that anywhere in my sales quotas.

b. I can answer that question, but it wouldn't be fair to nickels and pennies.

c. I do not stand on quotas; I am usually under them. A lot. All the time.

d. Sales quotas are not fair because I cannot find time to pay bills, run errands, and talk on the telephone if I have to worry about making a certain number of sales. When am I supposed to take a nap? When am I supposed to surf the Internet? Where is the justice in this? Isn't this a free country? How am I supposed to find time to drop off and pick up my dry cleaning? All these suits can think about are their quotas—where is the humanity?

4. A good day at the office generally includes:

a. A nap.

b. No responsibilities or interruptions.

c. Both a and b.

d. All of the above.

SCORING:

Sigh...

4–6: You know the drill, but you are treading on thin ice. If you're gonna be a slacker, you gotta quit the yapping and get with the napping.

7–9: Okay, Clueless Wonder, how did you get this job? Here's some news for you: the FCC is not doing away with religious programming; Abercrombie & Fitch is not sending you free clothes for forwarding their e-mail; and the reason it seems everybody knows "somebody who knows somebody" who brought a Mexican rat to the States because they thought it was a dog is because *the story is not true—you are just gullible.*

10–12: We're too exhausted after ranting on that last one to score this one.

13–16: Your approach to productivity is practical. It's not that you don't care about your company; you just don't feel like contributing to it. Other things need your attention: your friends, your pets, your friends, your clothes, and your friends. After reviewing this list, you discover that you actually accomplish quite a bit during the workday—there's just very little time left to actually work.

Team-building Ideas:

A rousing game of "Hide the HR Files" can waken even the deepest office slumber. Rearrange as many files as you can and then wait quietly to hear the bewildered expletives pour forth.

Conduct a cobweb contest. See who can grow the longest cobweb on their telephone receiver. Winner gets a free dinner, compliments of petty cash or the stamp fund.

PRODUCTIVITY IS: 10% CONFUSION, 90% ILLUSION. AND FACTOR IN A LARGE MARGIN OF ERROR, FOR GOODNESS' SAKE.

A Fable Run A-Fowl

Every morning in America, a chicken wakes up. It knows it must run faster than the fastest fox or it will be killed. Every morning a fox wakes up. It knows it must outrun the slowest chicken or it will starve to death. It doesn't matter whether you are a fox or a chicken—when the sun comes up, you'd better be running or somebody's goose'll be cooked by lunchtime.

On Sales Reports:

There's a reason sales are reported in terms of units; otherwise, you'd have to report how many of your friends received the employee discount and how much of the stuff you simply gave away.

SUBLIMINAL MESSAGE:
Production. Product? Shun. Hmmmm...

ASK NO QUESTIONS. TELL NO LIES.
Well, unless it's about your sales
quotas or expense reports.

From the *Glossary of Professional Terms*:
Uncall: *n.* or *v.* 1. A call knowingly made when someone is away from the office, usually because you really don't want to talk to that person. 2. To make contact when you are fairly certain you will get the person's voicemail.

Examples: *If you don't have an answer for the client, you can always make an* **uncall**.

Sally meant to **uncall** *Bill, but he was still in the building and was paged—so she didn't get away with it.*

One dark and stormy night...

an elderly farmer in a quaint village was cutting out early from his greeter job at a discount superstore in a nearby town. He noticed they were nailing the entrance to the All-Nite Wool 'n' Day-ree (and Now Cars, Too!) closed. His truck sputtered over to the curb, and the farmer called, "Hey! What's going on?"

"We're closing for good," explained the woman, hiding her face and feeling ashamed. Granted, it had been a while, but she still didn't want the farmer to recognize her. "We should have never gotten into the car business. The cows and sheep felt shunned, and now they're all calling in sick, claiming that the place smells funny and that they all have hoof-and-mouth disease. We can't prove it, but we strongly suspect it's a sick-in."

Productivity is chaff without good employee relations.

SUCCESS

After clawing your way to the top,
get used to your new title:
#1 Lightning Rod.

SUCCESS

The Joy of the Journey

What defines success? Is it a journey or a destination? Success is always about the journey—so long as it's navigated by your limo driver.

Have you ever noticed how people who are loaded will tell you, "It's not about the money"??? Let's get this straight: Pay no attention to those people. Either they were born into great wealth and therefore do not know any better, or they have clawed and stomped on enough people to accumulate the wealth that they have and have lost all sense of what is right and wrong in the process. Okay, okay—maybe it's not *all* about the money, but wouldn't it be nice to find out for sure???

The beautiful things. The beautiful friends. The beautiful children. The home, car, and collection of grown-up "toys" that are all part of this journey to success. You may step on a few toes along the way, but learn to justify your actions and excuse your way out of these unpleasantries— just as your predecessors did to you. It's all a part of the circle of life (not to be confused with the gerbil wheel upon which you're currently scampering). What's the use of chasing a dream, after all, if it cannot be caught?

Your steps may be tiny in some places (blame everything on Ethel to ensure that she doesn't get ahead, ahead of you) and huge in others (letting juicy information accidentally-on-purpose "slip" into the right hands). Whatever the size of your steps to success, decorate them with fabulous vacations and expensive treats. Be mindful to stay a jump ahead of the rest of your beautiful friends. Make others envious of your calculated, fabricated life—it's the American way.

And remember, when you count yourself as having "arrived," don't get too comfy—you won't be there long.

Very often, the beautiful people got that way through the hard work of a creative plastic surgeon.

A Table of Measurement for So-called Adults

They say success cannot be measured, but we beg to differ—here's a little chart for all you scorekeepers out there.

By Age...	You should have...	And if not, then...
18	Enrolled in college and/or secured a job in retail. And a BMW.	Marry well. Or buy a BMW keychain and park your '78 Nova several blocks away.
22	A college degree and/or a retail management position. A brand, spanking-new Beemer.	Marry well, 'cause the retail thing is a real downer. And lease a BMW to celebrate your new prestige as a manager...um, okay, *assistant* manager.
25	A job as an assistant (to someone powerful) that pays you peanuts. A chic apartment in the "right" neighborhood.	Act like a bigshot, despite the fact that you are driving a car you cannot afford. Rent a P.O. Box in the "right" neighborhood so everyone'll think you live there.
28	Blown the whistle on the shiftiness of your boss. The company will be so indebted you'll be promoted to Vice President of Everything. Use new salary to purchase swank home in "right" neighborhood.	Rent some smelly hole-in-the-wall in the "right" neighborhood. Find a bus schedule because you're dumb enough to still be leasing a car that rarely runs properly. You'll start having visions of having to work for the rest of your life—but at least you've been promoted to manager.
31	Dampened the spirits and dashed the hopes of every coworker who's younger or in a lower position than you. Get shifty boss's old job. Add new wing to swank home to celebrate.	Vent frustration to landlord that you're still paying over-priced rent and the rodents aren't chipping in. Quit the retail scene, get job at nameless, faceless company. Take blackmail notes from the personal phone calls of the entry-level flunky in the next cube.
34	Freedom to play golf two afternoons a week, and slack off the other three. Time to purchase a boat and consider early retirement.	Blackmail notes should pay off in the form of a nicer office than most. You deserve it because you didn't marry well and therefore can spend more time there.
40	An SUV so you won't mess up the Mercedes. Semi-retirement is a beautiful thing.	Purchase a decent used car that is new to you. Dream of early retirement.
42	Aw, who needs to work as long as the checks keep rolling in? Purchase an Italian villa to celebrate retirement.	Some sort of home to call your own. Keep working on that early retirement scheme.
47	A dog and a private plane (you're taking lessons).	Marry well (the best early retirement plan you can come up with).

Cling-on, Office Whine-O

Common title: Changes so often, one cannot keep up.

Identified by: All the personal problems that beset his/her life. Cling-on spends workdays either on the phone arguing with significant other, friends, children, etc., or whining to coworkers about significant other, friends, children, etc. Most of the time, however, Cling-on cannot come to work because there are issues and/or illnesses involving significant other, friends, children, etc. Cling-on brings practically every illness into the office by either coming to work ill and contagious or dragging his/her sick children into work. It's Cling-on's way of spreading misery and showing how devoted he/she is to the company. Famous for saying, "Well, enough about me, what do you think of me?"

Best trait: Makes all other employees look good; Cling-on's life also reminds you that you're not the loser you thought you were. Cling-on's enjoying a one-way trip to Nowheresville. In a weird way, Cling-on gives you hope that someday you will be promoted.

Worst trait: Cling-on's cube is on the other side of yours, so you're either listening to Hagasaurus or catching Cling-on's latest infection/problem. Get working on that promotion, pronto.

A penny saved is a penny yearned, come April 15th.

Nuggets O'Wisdom

On the road to success, you can be sure of one thing—bad drivers.

Countless, unseen details are often the only difference between mediocre and "looks like we got away with it."

Some people dream of success, while others wake up and work hard for those people.

Wisdom is knowing what path to take next. Pure genius is charting a shortcut and stopping for lunch along the way.

This is the beginning of a new day. You have been given this day to use as you will. You can waste it or use it for good. What you do today is important because you are exchanging a day of your life for it. When tomorrow comes, this day will be gone forever, a day that is either lost or well-spent. Days are important, yessiree. There are rainy days, sunny days, snowy days, windy days. And if your day is ordinary, well that is a day that is a day just like any other day, except for those days that are bad or those days that are exceptionally good, but how often does that come in this day and age?!

Start each day by breathing in, calmly and deeply. Unless, of course, you live near a fertilizer factory.

From the *Glossary of Professional Terms*:
Average day: *n.* When you excel in all areas of employment, including attendance, work ethic, honesty, and performance, yet remain ignored until the one time you falter—say, a personal call or longer lunch than usual—and then you are busted.

Example: *It was just another **average day** at the office.*

One dark and stormy night...

an elderly farmer in a quaint village was thinking about the production and destruction he'd experienced since the terrible storm that ultimately took his farm and livelihood away.

He'd seen a lot come and go since then: The All-Nite Wool 'n' Day-ree had gone from a milk and wool boutique to a major dairy, wool, and car dealership to bankruptcy court; his prized horse, once regarded as a beautiful animal, had yukked his way to ruin by running with a wild crowd; and then there was his truck, which sputtered and spattered but never stalled. "Lots of changes," he whispered to himself.

"I've managed to make a living on the tips from hauling people around in my truck. And I've managed to save a bit of money from my job as a greeter at the discount superstore. Maybe I should consider starting my own business. I can't be a greeter and a makeshift taxi driver forever."

Walking into town, he noticed a "For Sale" sign at the old wool/dairy/car shop that still smelled funny and still had that eerie glow, even though it had been vacant for a while. And suddenly, a lightbulb came on inside his feeble brain.

The next morning the once-prized horse awoke, tiptoed out the back door (lest the elderly farmer need a ride somewhere), and went for a stroll, only to find the "For Sale" sign removed from the wool and dairy shop. Instead, he found the "For Sale" sign on the front gate of the farm, along with a note, which read:

Dear Prized Horse,
Have moved to Bermuda. This place is becoming less and less quaint;
besides, it is too dark and stormy here.
Best of luck,
The elderly farmer

The once-prized horse galloped over to the "All-Nite," where the other "For Sale" sign had been. Attached to the building was a note, which read:

Dear Prized Horse,
Did you really think I'd buy this place? It sits on top of an old toxic
waste dump. I may be simple, but I ain't stupid.
Best of luck,
The elderly farmer

Wonder who bought the place, thought the horse. Inside, the buyers stood on their hooves, marveling that a pack of wild horses successfully managed to secure a business loan.

"To teamwork!" they toasted.

Your Secret Office Code Name:

Everyone at work has a nickname whether they know it or not.
Use the chart on the right to name yourself before someone else
tags you. We'll use the author's name as an example: Miriam Drennan.
Here's how it works:

1. Match the first letter of your first name with the corresponding
   word in Column 1.
   example: Miriam Drennan   M= Smarty

2. Next, match the last letter of your first name with the corresponding
   word in Column 2.
   example: Miriam Drennan   M= Keyboard

3. Finally, match the last letter of your last name with the
   corresponding word in Column 3.
   example: Miriam Drennan   N= Pants

Put them together and you'll be surprised how accurate
and effective this naming system can be!

Miriam's Secret Office Code Name is:
Smarty Keyboard Pants

Some famous people's names:
George W. Bush: Giggly Calculator Face
Michael J. Fox: Smarty Pink Slip Shorts
Donald Trump: Brainy Hard Drive Lips
Leona Helmsley: Scary Stapler Freak
Ted Turner: Winkie Hard Drive Nostril
Hillary Clinton: Sneaky Ruler Pants
Frank Sinatra: Snappy Toilet Paper Noggin
Bill Gates: Smoochie Pink Slip Bucket

Column 1: The first letter of your first name.	Column 2: The last letter of your first name.	Column 3: The last letter of your last name.
A. Snuggly	A. Stapler	A. Noggin
B. Smoochie	B. Mouse Pad	B. Britches
C. Grumpy	C. Paper Clip	C. Head
D. Brainy	D. Hard Drive	D. Butt
E. Puffy	E. Calculator	E. Arm Pit
F. Snappy	F. Swivel Chair	F. Fingers
G. Giggly	G. Ball-Point	G. Earlobe
H. Sneaky	H. Sticky Note	H. Face
I. Mean Ol'	I. Rest Room	I. Buttocks
J. Softy	J. Fine Point	J. Knuckles
K. Wimpy	K. Toilet Paper	K. Kook
L. Scary	L. Pink Slip	L. Cheeks
M. Smarty	M. Keyboard	M. Hot Pants
N. Chunky	N. High Lighter	N. Pants
O. Frownie	O. Red Ink	O. Cranium
P. Poopy	P. Pencil Lead	P. Lips
Q. Squishy	Q. Day Timer	Q. Rear End
R. Laughie	R. Disc Drive	R. Nostril
S. Slurpy	S. Coffee Pot	S. Bucket
T. Winkie	T. Duct Tape	T. Blow Hole
U. Snoozy	U. Scotch Tape	U. Mouth
V. Hefty	V. Masking Tape	V. Belly
W. Stinky	W. Potty Break	W. Toe Jam
X. Tiny	X. Elevator	X. Shorts
Y. Kissy	Y. Ruler	Y. Freak
Z. Floppy	Z. Sippy Cup	Z. Knee Cap

Your Secret Office Code Name is:

_____   _____   _____

Miriam Drennan is pretty much a nobody who happened to be working at the right place at the right time and landed a cool writing assignment from her boss, Joel. Being an expert on the subject matter, Miriam merely assembled about ten years' worth of her research findings. Now that the thing has been published, Miriam is back at work, hard at work trying to avoid having to work.

When she's not drooling at her desk, Miriam is the sole benefactor to some wild, four-legged beast named Abbey who claims to be a dog with a promising tap-dancing career. Whatever.

Some of the proceeds from this book will go to the Pay Miriam's Mortgage fund, a very worthy cause.

Joel Anderson is also a nobody, albeit a more successful one. Joel is cofounder of Anderson Thomas Design (a really cool graphic design firm that can handle anything—they even designed this whole book—so please call them for all your print and web design needs).

One day, he noticed Miriam drooling at her desk. Remembering that he paid a portion of her insurance premiums, he thought it would be best that she write out her feelings instead of hiring some expensive therapist to straighten her out. What you hold in your hands is proof that journaling is cheaper than therapy.

When he is not busy shooting rubberbands at his employees, Joel enjoys gardening and spending time with his wife (who is actually quite normal) and their three sons.